Mummies

Modern Mummies:

20th-Century Wonders and Beyond

by **Michael Martin**

Consultant:

Dr. Salima Ikram

Department of Egyptology

American University in Cairo

Cairo, Egypt

Capstone *press*

Mankato, Minnesota

Edge Books are published by Capstone Press,
151 Good Counsel Drive, P.O. Box 669, Mankato, Minnesota 56002.
www.capstonepress.com

Library of Congress Cataloging-in-Publication Data
Martin, Michael, 1948–
   Modern mummies: 20th-century wonders and beyond / by Michael Martin.
     p. cm.—(Edge Books, mummies)
   Includes bibliographical references and index.
   ISBN 0-7368-3771-X (hardcover)
   1. Mummies. I. Title. II. Series.
GN293.M36 2005
393'.3—dc22   2004012374

Summary: Describes mummies from the 1900s, as well as how scientists use modern
techniques to make mummies today.

Editorial Credits
Carrie A. Braulick, editor; Kia Adams, set designer; Jennifer Bergstrom, book designer;
   Kelly Garvin, photo researcher; Scott Thoms, photo editor

Photo Credits
AP/Wide World Photos/Eric Stocklin, 29; Sergei Karpukhin, 7
Brian T. Ezzelle, Richmond, VA, 19
Corbis/Bettmann, 14; Steve Raymer, 10
Getty Images Inc., 8; Hulton Archive, cover, 4, 12, 25; Time Life Pictures, 20
Kimberly A. King, 23
Photo courtesy of Alcor Life Extension Foundation, 2004, 26
Photo courtesy of Christine Quigley, 16, 22
Western History Collections, University of Oklahoma Library, 18

**Capstone Press thanks Arthur C. Aufderheide, MD, Department of Pathology
and Laboratory Medicine, University of Minnesota, Duluth, for his assistance
in preparing this book.**

Table of Contents

Learn About:

- Vladimir Lenin's mummy
- Types of modern mummies
- George Mallory's mummy

In March 1924, Russian scientists were asked to make Vladimir Lenin's body into a mummy.

Chapter One

Making a Modern Mummy

In March 1924, two Russian scientists received a strange job. They had to preserve a dead body so it looked exactly as it had in life. Boris Zbarsky and Vladimir Vorobiov knew their job wouldn't be easy. Russian leaders were depending on the scientists to do a good job. For the next four months, they slept and ate next to the body as they completed their work.

The body belonged to Vladimir Lenin. Lenin had been Russia's first leader under communism. He died in January 1924.

At the time, even the best ways to preserve a body didn't work perfectly. Part of the body's tissues still decayed. But Russian leaders still wanted Zbarsky and Vorobiov's work to last forever.

The Russian scientists did a good job. When they were finished, Lenin appeared to be sleeping peacefully. Russian leaders were happy. They put Lenin's mummy in a glass-topped case at the Lenin Mausoleum in Moscow. Today, many people still visit the mausoleum to see his mummy.

Today, Lenin's body still looks as it did when he died in 1924.

A Famous Modern Ice Mummy

In 1999, mountain climbers made one of the most famous modern mummy discoveries. The body belonged to mountain climber George Mallory.

In 1924, Mallory disappeared on Mount Everest. Mallory was trying to become the first person to climb the mountain. Its 29,035-foot (8,850-meter) peak makes it the world's highest mountain. Mount Everest lies in the Himalayan mountain range in southern Asia. The cold conditions on the mountain preserved Mallory's body.

The climbers who found Mallory's body couldn't bring it down the mountain. Air at the top of Mount Everest has little oxygen. Carrying extra weight wouldn't allow the climbers to breathe enough oxygen. Instead, the climbers held a short ceremony. Mallory's mummy still lies in its resting place.

Mallory's mummy

About Modern Mummies

Some of the most well-known mummies are hundreds or thousands of years old. By studying these mummies, scientists have learned how past societies lived. Scientists often spend less time studying modern mummies. But these mummies also can help scientists learn about the past.

Modern mummies are made in several ways. Some mummies are made on purpose. Scientists have made mummies of government leaders to honor them. Some people choose to become mummies after they die. They hope future scientific discoveries will bring their bodies back to life. Natural conditions preserve other bodies. Modern mummies have been found in water, ice, and deserts.

Learn About:

- Displaying the dead
- Secret methods
- Josef Stalin's mummy

Today, people still visit the building that holds Vietnam's past communist leader, Ho Chi Minh.

Chapter Two

Communist Mummies

Russia was the first country to make mummies of its communist leaders. Russians often visited the mummies. Soon, leaders of other communist countries also wanted to put their dead leaders on display.

Making Lenin's Mummy

The exact steps Zbarsky and Vorobiov used to preserve Lenin's body are still a secret.

Russian leaders put Josef Stalin on display just after he died.

EDGE FACT

So many people came to see Stalin's body that several people were trampled to death.

Only some parts of the process are known. The scientists put certain chemicals inside the body. They bathed the body in other chemicals. They removed mold that had already formed on the skin.

Few communist mummies are as well preserved as Lenin's mummy. Scientists from other countries who tried to copy Zbarsky and Vorobiov's process weren't always successful.

Josef Stalin

Josef Stalin became Russia's communist leader after Lenin. Stalin died in 1953. Russian leaders asked Zbarsky to preserve Stalin's body. When Zbarsky finished, Stalin looked like he was sleeping. The mummy was dressed in a military uniform.

Russian leaders placed Stalin's mummy next to Lenin's mummy in the mausoleum. But Stalin was not popular with Russia's later leaders. In 1962, they took away Stalin's mummy and buried it.

Other Communist Mummies

Mao Tse-tung became the communist leader of China in 1948. When he died in 1976, leaders decided to mummify his body.

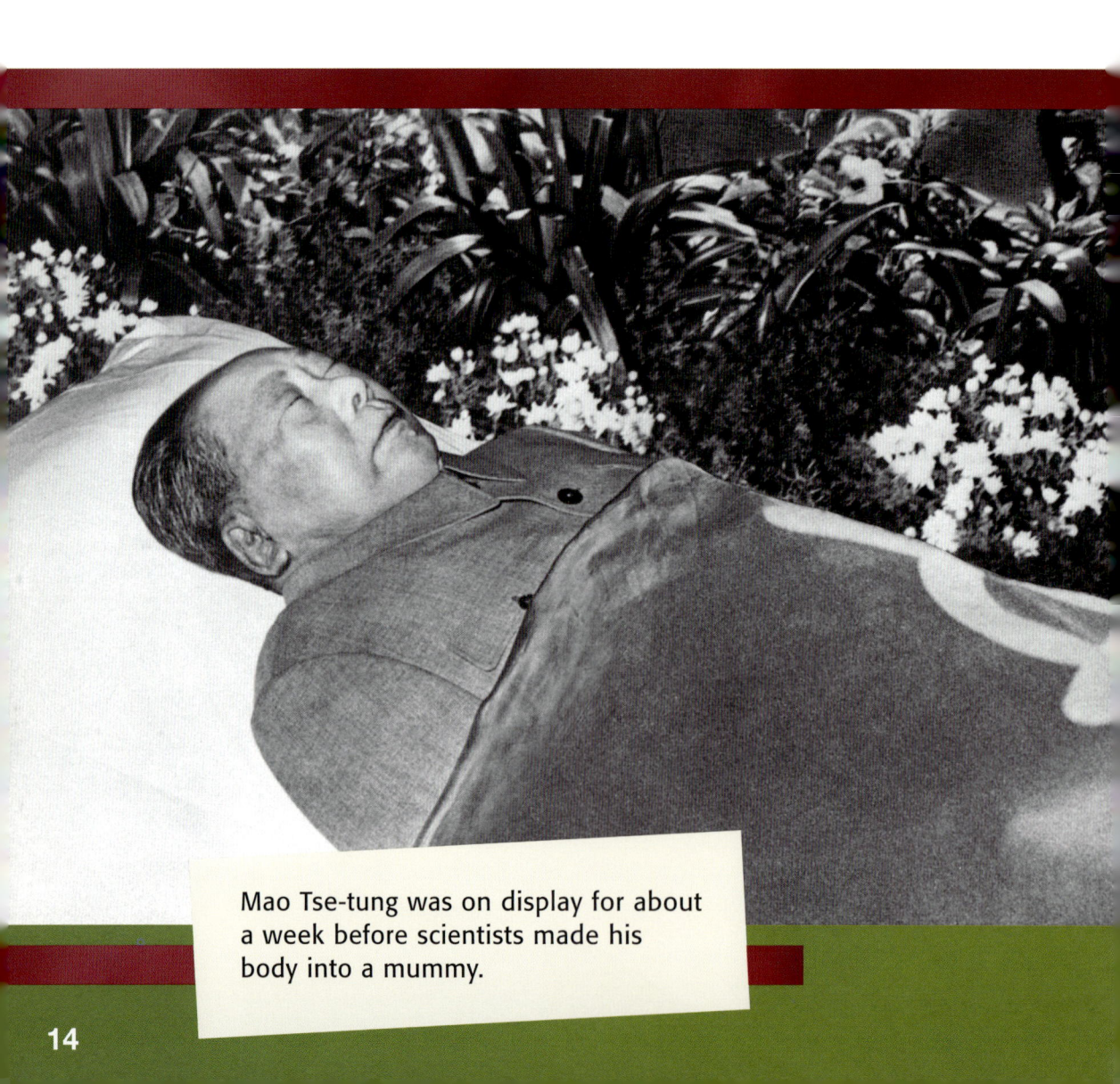

Mao Tse-tung was on display for about a week before scientists made his body into a mummy.

Mao's body was still swollen when scientists wanted to put him on display. His suit wouldn't fit him. The scientists cut the suit so they could dress him in it.

Chinese scientists knew little about making mummies. They did a poor job. Too many chemicals made Mao's face swell and his ears stick out. It took more work to make Mao's face look normal.

Today, Mao's mummy is displayed in a mausoleum in Tiananmen Square in Beijing, China. The mummy shows its age. The face is wrinkled and the body is discolored.

Past communist leaders Ho Chi Minh of Vietnam and Kim Il Sung of North Korea also are preserved as mummies. Both of these mummies are on display. Ho Chi Minh's mummy rests in a tomb in Hanoi, Vietnam. Kim Il Sung's mummy is in the Kumsusan Memorial Palace in Pyongyang, North Korea.

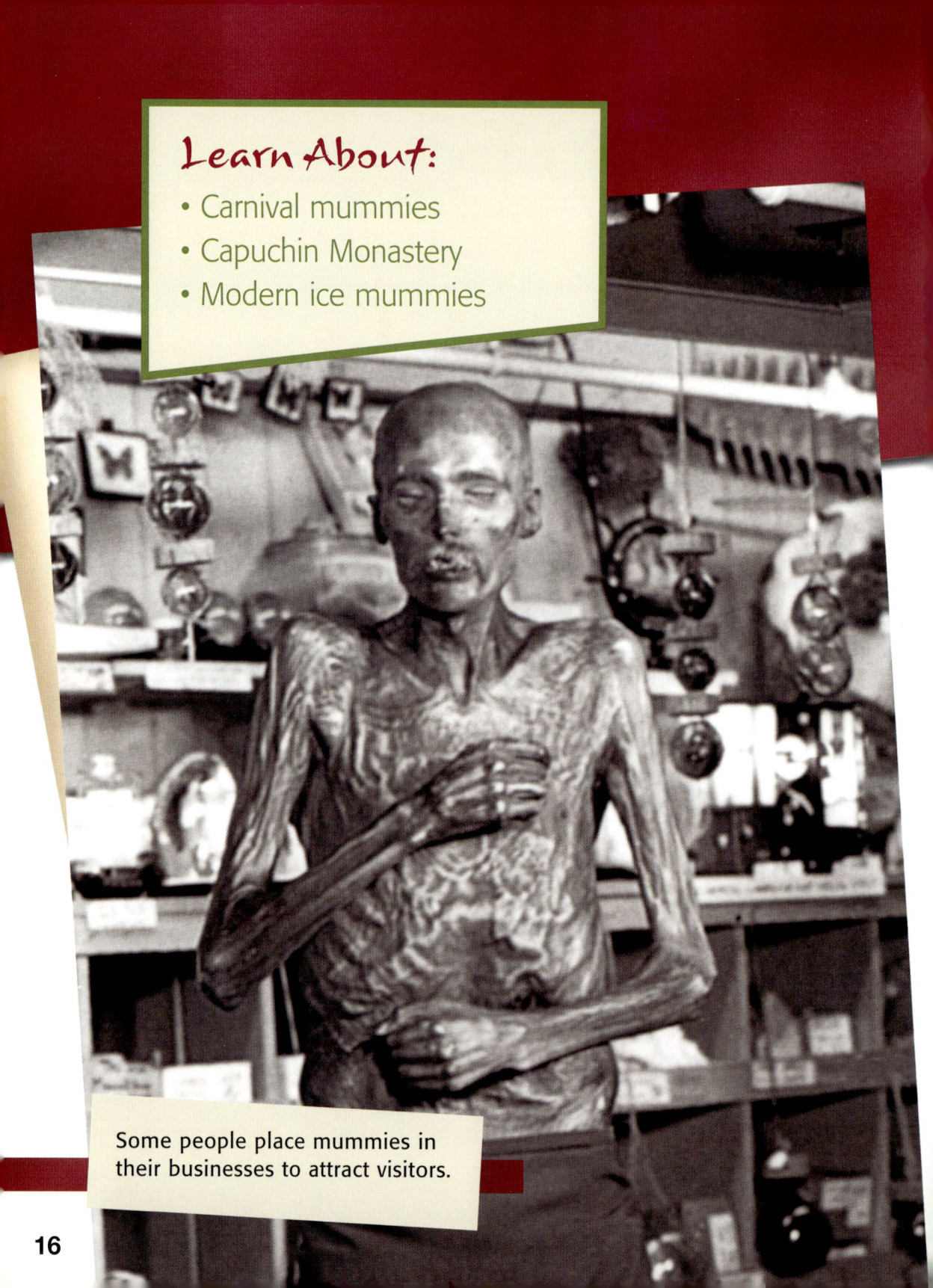

Learn About:
- Carnival mummies
- Capuchin Monastery
- Modern ice mummies

Some people place mummies in their businesses to attract visitors.

Chapter Three

Mummies among Us

Many communist mummies are still cared for so they keep a lifelike appearance. Other modern mummies are in much worse condition. But even these mummies can attract thousands of curious visitors.

Elmer McCurdy

In 1911, Elmer McCurdy robbed a train in Oklahoma. He later died in a shoot-out with police.

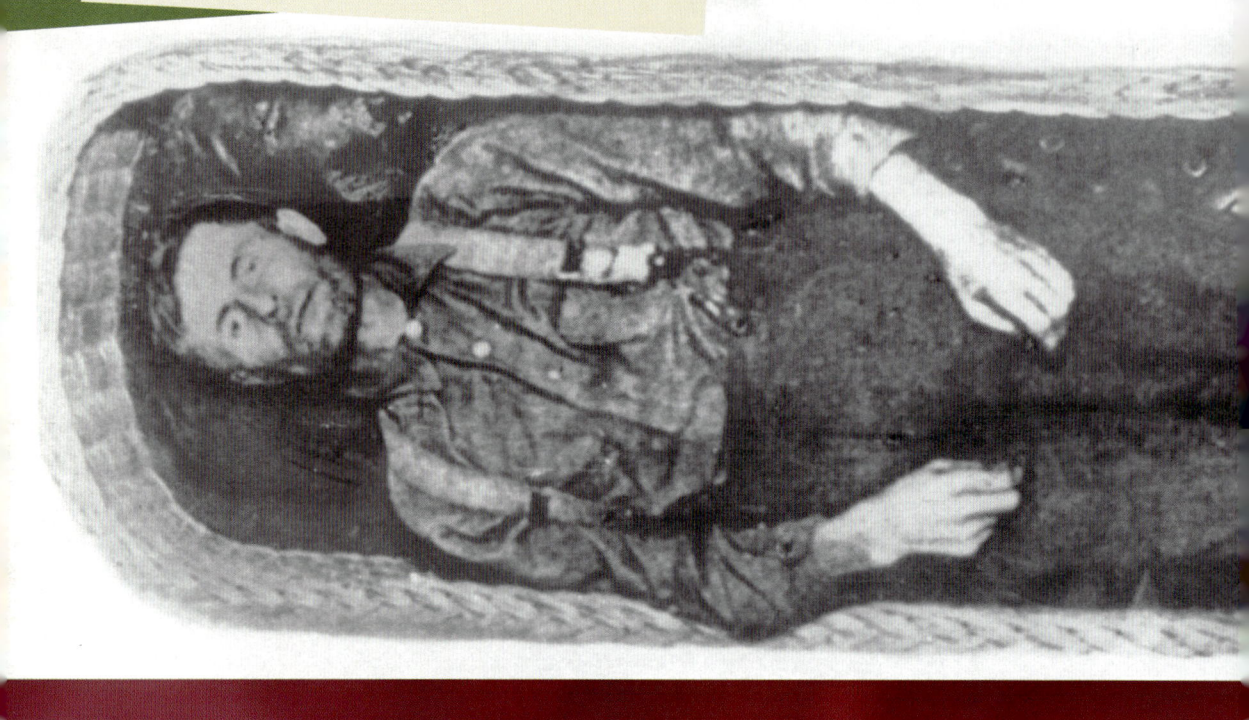

Elmer McCurdy's history as an outlaw made him popular as a carnival mummy.

A funeral director embalmed McCurdy's body. He treated it with chemicals to keep the body from decaying. People usually bury a body a few days after it is embalmed. But no one came to claim McCurdy's body. The body dried out and turned into a mummy.

The funeral director charged people money to see it. Later, a traveling carnival displayed McCurdy's mummy for several years.

Marie O'Day

Marie O'Day was a nightclub entertainer in Utah. She disappeared in the mid-1920s. O'Day's husband was arrested for killing her. Although the body had not been found yet, he was sent to prison for the crime.

In 1937, O'Day's body was found in Utah's Great Salt Lake. The salt in the water had preserved her body. Carnival workers then toured the United States and Canada with O'Day's mummy.

Salt water preserved Marie O'Day's body.

Today, many people still want to know
if this mummy is John Wilkes Booth
or if it is someone else.

Some people think mummies are cursed. The John Wilkes Booth mummy seems to have brought bad luck. Most people who owned the mummy went broke. In 1902, a train carrying the mummy crashed. Eight people were killed in the crash.

John Wilkes Booth

A mystery surrounds the carnival mummy named John Wilkes Booth. In 1865, Booth shot U.S. President Abraham Lincoln. Most people believe that soldiers later killed Booth. A few people think he escaped.

Carnival owners claimed to display Booth's mummy in the early 1900s. But some people think the mummy was actually of David E. George. George had claimed to be Booth until he died in 1903.

Hazel Farris

In 1907, carnival owners bought a mummy named Hazel Farris. A story said that Farris shot and killed her husband and four other men in Kentucky in 1905. She then swallowed poison to kill herself.

In 2002, college professors Ronald Beckett and Gerald Conlogue made a TV show about mummies. They studied the mummy of Hazel Farris. Beckett and Conlogue believe the story about the murders may be untrue. They think Farris died from the lung disease pneumonia.

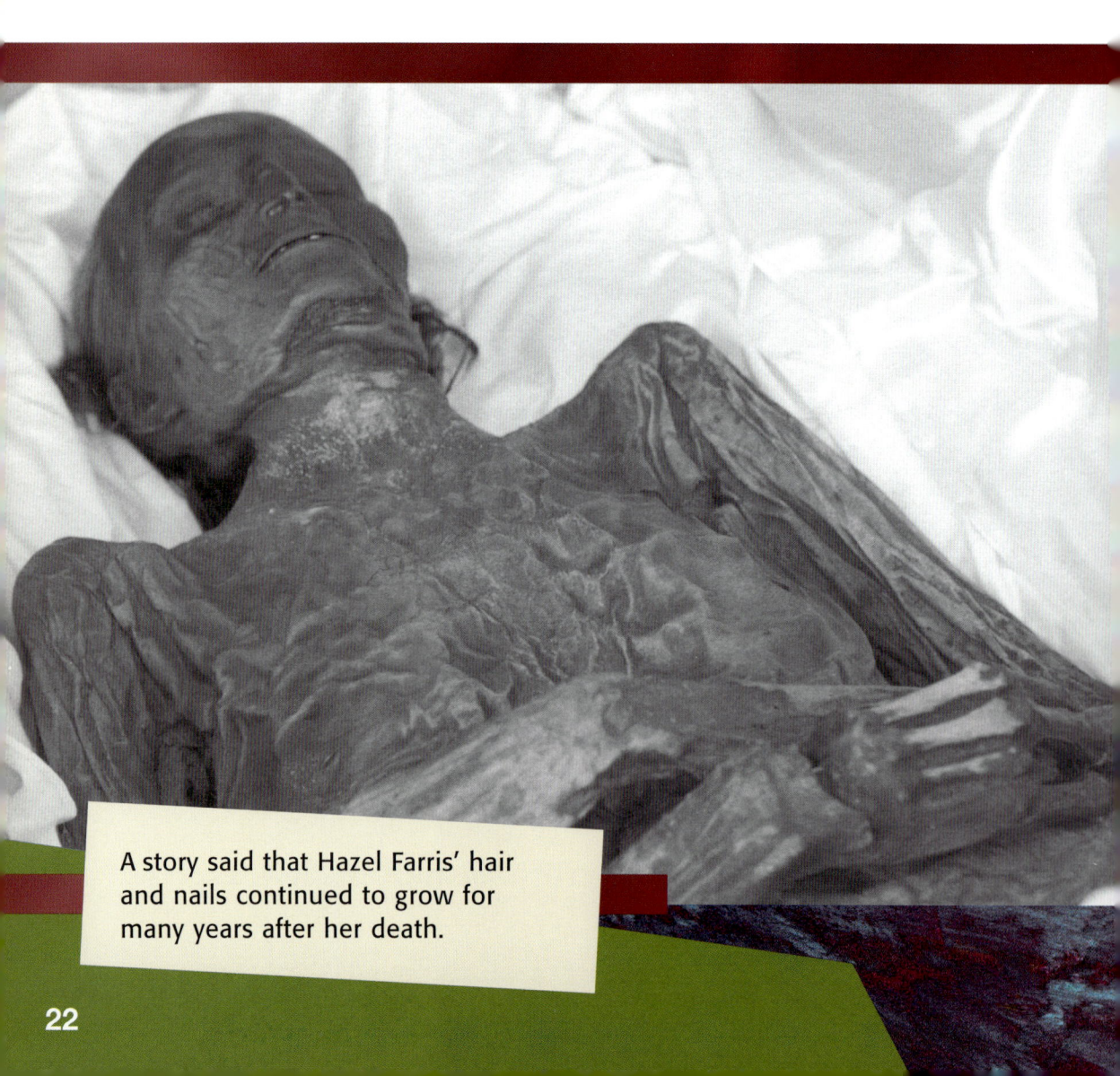

A story said that Hazel Farris' hair and nails continued to grow for many years after her death.

Rosalia Lombardo

In 1920, 2-year-old Rosalia Lombardo died in Italy. Dr. Alfredo Salafia used strong chemicals to embalm her body. Salafia's embalming fluid preserved bodies longer than other fluids. Salafia kept the chemicals he used in the fluid a secret.

Lombardo's mummy was one of the last mummies placed in the Capuchin Monastery in Palermo, Italy. The mummy joined many others being kept there by the monks.

Today, Lombardo's body looks like it did when she died. Most of the other mummies in the monastery have dried out or shrunk. People call Lombardo "Sleeping Beauty."

Lombardo's mummy is slightly yellow, but it has not decayed.

Eva Peron

Eva Peron became one of the most famous modern mummies. She died in 1953. Her husband, Juan Peron, asked a doctor to preserve her body. At the time, Peron was president of Argentina. Peron put his wife's mummy on display in a glass-topped coffin. In 1955, Argentina's military took over the government. Soldiers took Eva Peron's body to Europe and buried it.

In 1973, Juan Peron again became Argentina's president. After his death in 1974, government leaders returned his wife's body to Argentina. The body had changed little since her death. In 1976, Eva Peron's body was buried in Buenos Aires, Argentina.

Modern Ice Mummies

Freezing temperatures can form ice mummies. Scientists found the oldest ice mummy in 1991. This mummy may be 5,000 years old. Other ice mummies formed much more recently.

Cold conditions on mountains preserve some bodies. In 1934, mountain climbers Henna Schlager and Josef Schneider never returned from a climb in the Alps. This mountain range lies in south-central Europe. Their bodies were found in 1991. In 1981, mountain climbing guide Kurt Jeschke died after a fall in the Alps. His body also was discovered in 1991.

In 1974, Eva Peron's body was placed next to her husband's coffin.

Learn About:
- Mummy-making businesses
- Freezing bodies
- Cost of making a mummy

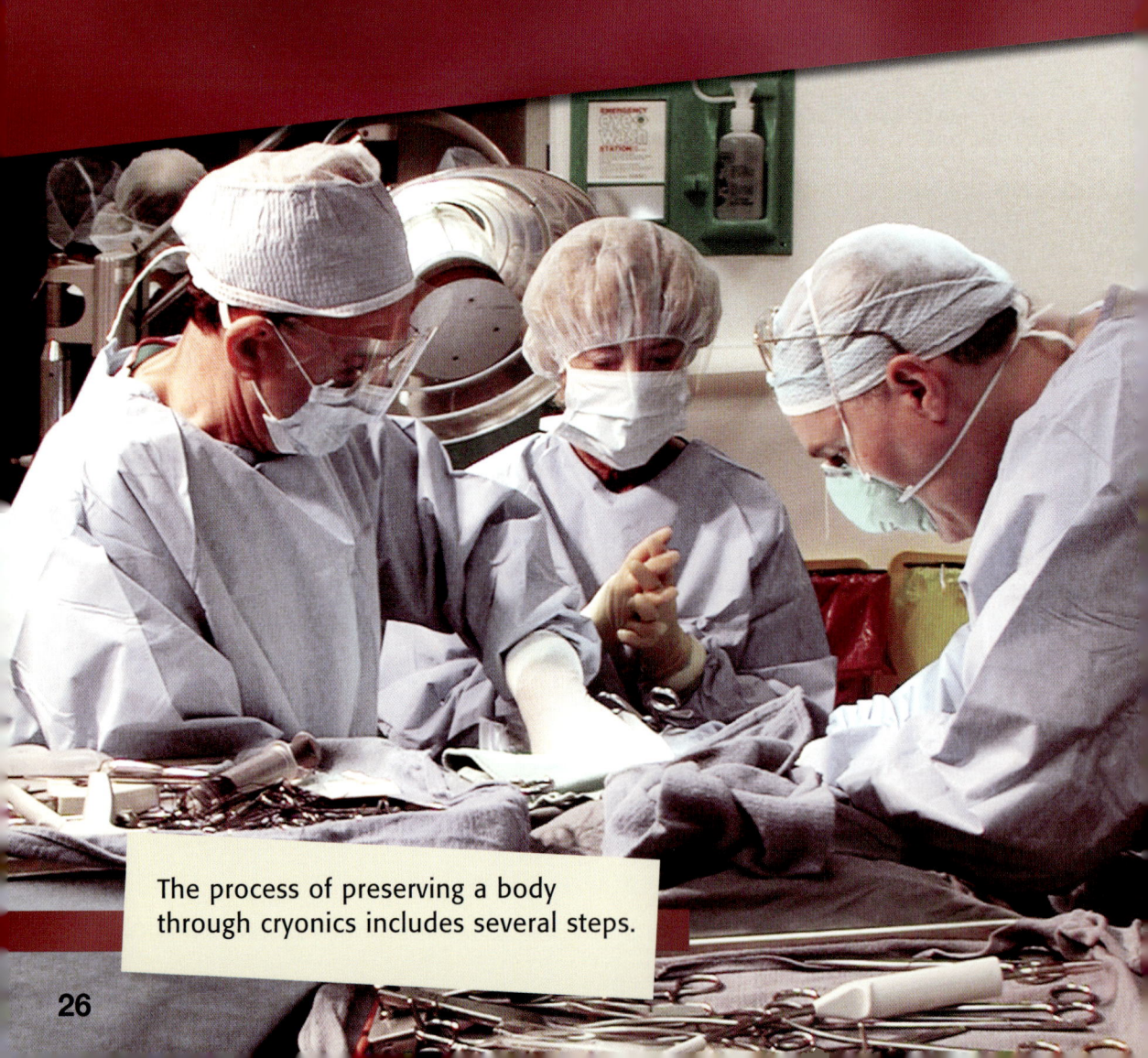

The process of preserving a body through cryonics includes several steps.

Chapter Four

Making Mummies Today

Today, some people choose to become mummies after death. Businesses that make mummies preserve several bodies each year.

Summum

A company called Summum makes mummies in Salt Lake City, Utah. The company charges about $67,000 to make a human mummy. Summum also makes mummies of pets for about $14,000.

Summmum workers follow several steps to make mummies. They bathe the bodies in chemicals. They wrap the bodies in layers of cloth and place them in a case. The cases are buried in a cemetery or kept in a storage building especially for mummies.

Cryonics

Cryonics is the most modern way to make mummies. Liquid nitrogen chills the body to minus 310 degrees Fahrenheit (minus 190 degrees Celsius). People who choose to be frozen by cryonics hope they can be thawed and returned to life someday.

Cryonics is costly. People usually pay about $120,000 to have their body frozen. People can have only their head frozen for about half that cost. These people hope their heads can be attached to another body before being brought back to life.

Many scientists doubt medical advances that bring bodies back to life will ever be made. Yet hundreds of people still plan to be frozen through cryonics after death.

Making an Ancient Egyptian Mummy

In 1994, scientists at the University of Maryland wanted to make a mummy the same way ancient Egyptians had. They used the body of a 76-year-old man for their experiment.

The scientists followed the ancient Egyptian process of making mummies as closely as they could. They used only tools of bronze or stone. They removed the body's brain and internal organs. They left the heart in place. The scientists washed out the body's insides with wine. They placed packets of salt inside the body. For 35 days, they stored the body in a warm, dry room. Afterward, the body looked very much like an ancient Egyptian mummy. Its weight had dropped from 150 pounds (68 kilograms) to 75 pounds (34 kilograms).

Three more months of drying caused the mummy to lose even more weight. The scientists wrapped the mummy in 20 pounds (9 kilograms) of cloth and placed it in a casket. It remains at the University of Maryland.

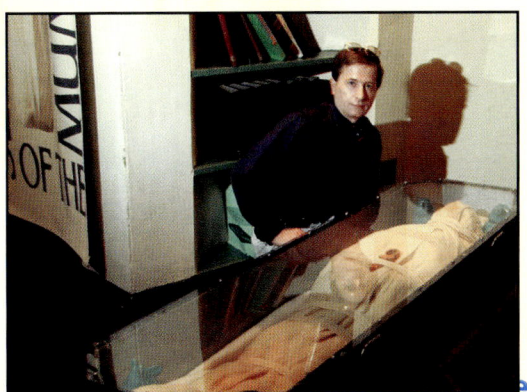

Glossary

communism (KOM-yuh-niz-uhm)—a way of organizing a country so that all property belongs to the government with profits being shared by all

decay (dee-KAY)—to break down or rot

embalm (im-BALM)—to preserve a dead body so it does not decay

liquid nitrogen (LIK-wid NYE-truh-juhn)—a liquid formed after nitrogen gas is pressurized and cooled

mausoleum (maw-suh-LEE-uhm)—a large building that holds tombs

monastery (MAH-nuh-ster-ee)—a group of buildings where monks live and work

organ (OR-guhn)—a part of the body that does a certain job

preserve (pree-ZURV)—to protect something so it stays in its original form

tissue (TISH-yoo)—a mass of cells that form a certain part or organ of a person, animal, or plant

Read More

Kallen, Stuart A. *Mummies.* Wonders of the World. San Diego: KidHaven Press, 2003.

MacDonald, Fiona. *Mysterious Mummies.* History Hunters. Milwaukee: Gareth Stevens, 2004.

Prior, Natalie Jane. *The Encyclopedia of Preserved People: Pickled, Frozen, and Mummified Corpses from around the World.* New York: Crown Publishers, 2003.

Internet Sites

FactHound offers a safe, fun way to find Internet sites related to this book. All of the sites on FactHound have been researched by our staff.

Here's how:

1. Visit *www.facthound.com*
2. Type in this special code **073683771X** for age-appropriate sites. Or enter a search word related to this book for a more general search.
3. Click on the **Fetch It** button.

FactHound will fetch the best sites for you!

Index